TRINITY CATHOLIC SCHOOL LIBRARY
706 EAST BREVARD STREET
TALLAHASSEE, FLORIDA 32303

W9-CEY-781

# ARMED WITH
# COURAGE

920
McM
C12

77-15

13144

# ARMED WITH
# COURAGE

by MAY McNEER and LYND WARD

*Nashville*　　ABINGDON PRESS　　*New York*

TRINITY CATHOLIC SCHOOL LIBRARY
706 EAST BREVARD STREET
TALLAHASSEE, FLORIDA 32303

Copyright © 1957 by Abingdon Press
All rights reserved
Lithographed in the United States of America
ISBN 0-687-01740-8

# CONTENTS

# Lady with a Lamp

## FLORENCE NIGHTINGALE

Florence glanced up from her Greek book and sighed. Such a long lesson Father had given her! Parthenope, her older sister, learned Greek easier than she did. And yet, thought Florence with a nod of satisfaction, I can do mathematics much better than she can! At sixteen Florence already knew far more Greek and Latin than most young men. She knew, also, the accomplishments of a rich young English lady. She could sing, embroider, paint flowers, and make jellies for the sick.

Florence gazed longingly through the window. There, on a peach bough, a small brown bird with a head as smooth as her own cocked his eye at her.

"Oh, how do you do, Mr. Nuthatch?" called Florence. "And how is your busy wife today?"

She jumped up, but paused at the door. If she left her Greek lesson unfinished, she would have to get up at four the next morning and study by cold lamplight. The pause was brief. Florence ran through the large house of the Nightingale family, into the gardens between rows of huge rhododendrons bearing pink blossoms above her head.

Beyond the lodges, stables, and gardens she stepped onto

the downs, stretching smooth and green to the hills. As Florence walked, her spirits rose. It was good to be on the downs in spring. Yet why did she have to do so much that she did not want to do? Why did she quarrel so often with Parthe? Florence knew that with her beauty and her bright mind she was Father's favorite. Parthe was jealous, no doubt. Florence enjoyed parties but often tired of the endless round of them that her mother insisted on. What did she want of life? She did not know — not yet —

Suddenly, as she came up over a hill, Florence saw a little knot of people. There with them was the pastor. Florence ran toward them calling, "Has someone been hurt?" Then she saw the dog lying on the grass. Old Shepherd Smithers turned and two farm boys pulled at their hair respectfully as the daughter of their squire appeared.

"Good morning, Miss Florence," said Reverend Gifford. "See, here is poor Cap, with a broken leg. He will have to be killed, I fear. Smithers' best collie, too."

Florence dropped to her knees. She stroked the rough head gently. Farm dogs were work animals and, like horses, were shot when they couldn't do their job. Florence loved all living creatures, from her old brown pony and her pet pig, to the tiny nuthatch swinging on the peach bough. The dog's brown eyes seemed to ask her for help. She spoke sharply.

"You must not kill Cap, Smithers. Pick him up — carefully now — and bring him to the stables. I will take care of him." There was a ringing tone of command in her voice.

At the stables the dog was made comfortable on a pile of straw. Florence washed the leg and bound it with a piece of wood

10

and clean old rags, and every day she came with food for Cap. It was the talk of the whole estate when the splint was removed and Cap walked on the mended leg again, without a limp.

Florence did not understand her own feelings. She could not read enough and learn enough to suit her. But she also liked parties, and lovely gowns, and she enjoyed being admired for her wit and beauty. Yet there was something else that meant much more to her. She could not forget the suffering eyes of the injured dog. She would always give up a party or miss a lesson to care for the sick children of the farmers. Florence wished that she could take care of all sick people — everywhere.

The daughters of Mr. and Mrs. Nightingale were born to riches. Their father, a country squire, was a learned man, and he taught his daughters himself. Their mother was a society leader. Florence had been named for the city of Florence, Italy, where she was born in 1820 during a year of travel for the

11

Nightingales, who often spent months at a time in Europe.

Yet, in the midst of every pleasure, Florence thought about the sick. She had a feeling that she had a mission in life and that she was meant to help sick people. She knew that her parents would not approve, so she sent secretly for every book and pamphlet that she heard of that told how to care for the sick. She read them late at night in her room, and whenever she went traveling to London, Rome, or Paris, she slipped away to visit hospitals. She must see for herself how bad they were.

The things that she saw were terrible. Sick people were lying in hospitals that were dens of noise and dirt. Even the doctors and nurses were seldom clean. Nobody had heard of germs, or of rows of white beds, neat and clean, or of sanitation to prevent disease. Well-to-do people, other than doctors, avoided all hospitals, which they thought were meant only for the poor.

After several years of this study, Florence's conversation proved that she knew more about the conditions in such places than almost anyone else did. Her relatives were dismayed. They could not understand her. Why didn't Flo marry one of the handsome gentlemen who admired her? complained Mrs. Nightingale. Mr. Nightingale was worried, too. Why, with her brilliant mind, wasn't Flo happy to be a scholar, as he was? When Florence asked permission to learn nursing, the horrified answer was "No!"

"Why, Flo," gasped Parthe, "hospital nurses are drunken women taken in from the streets."

Every time that Florence mentioned the subject, her mother had a "spell" of sickness and asked Flo to take care of

her. Florence visited the sick on the Nightingale estates, Lea Hurst and Embley. But she was unhappy. She went abroad again with family friends. In Paris she met brilliant people, and in Switzerland she got acquainted with scholarly refugees from Italy. From them she learned of the revolution going on there. She became ill and was invited to travel to Egypt, with friends. From there they went to Greece.

One day in Athens Florence found a tiny baby owl on the steps of the ruins of the Parthenon. She called it Athena, and when it was tamed it often rode about perched on her shoulder.

A Protestant religious hospital had been established in an ancient town on the River Rhine, in Germany. Florence longed to enter Kaiserswerth and be trained for nursing. Her traveling friends disliked leaving her there, but finally consented. This was something new to Florence—a clean hospital, where decent

13

women nursed the sick. All of the other nurses were working women, but no other nurse had ever learned to care for the sick so quickly and with such eagerness and skill as Florence Nightingale.

At the end of October Florence returned to England and her angry family. She faced the disgrace firmly. Now she really knew what she wanted to do. She intended to reform the hospitals of England! Yet, for a number of years, she could do nothing. Her mother, or aunts, or cousins begged her to nurse them in their illnesses. She took over the management of her family household and found that she had real talent for handling the many details of such a job. She did not know it at the time, but every one of these jobs helped prepare her for her later work.

Florence heard of a small hospital for women in London that needed a superintendent. She was thirty-three years old when she told her parents that she now meant to make her own decisions. Mrs. Nightingale cried, and Parthe cried, and all of the aunts and cousins cried. Mr. Nightingale argued with Flo and said that such work would probably kill her. But he did not actually refuse his permission, and she went to London as she had intended to do, with or without it. When Flo moved into the small hospital, her mother said with a sigh, "At least this is a respectable hospital for sick gentlewomen."

As head of the hospital Florence worked day and night. First she had the house thoroughly cleaned. Then she put everything in order and replenished supplies. Then she ordered medicines, and when the correct ones were not sent, she spoke to the chemist like a queen to a disobedient subject. When the council

14

of ladies who ran the hospital quarreled, Miss Nightingale brought them to terms. Then—at last—the hospital was running well, and Florence was—at last—doing the work that she wanted to do.

Sometimes she went home for a visit to Lea Hurst, and she enjoyed the parties as if she had never been away. She loved to be with the many babies and children always visiting there, and in the evening she entertained guests with her mimicry and fun.

In the autumn of 1854, England was thrown into excitement by the outbreak of war with Russia. Troops of both England and France were embarking for the Crimea, a peninsula that juts into the Black Sea north of Turkey. Florence Nightingale heard the news with great interest. She read every account of the landing of troops, and of the hospitals being set up at Scutari, across the Straits of Marmora from Constantinople. She read that soldiers were dying by hundreds with wounds untended. She immediately went to the Minister of War, who was an old friend, and offered to enlist nurses to take to Scutari.

Who had ever heard of such a thing? The Nightingales were so horrified that they could scarcely speak of it. But Florence set

15

out with her group of nurses, gathered from the best London hospitals and from some religious orders. A long trip by ship around and into the Mediterranean Sea, when waves tossed the vessel about and made them all seasick, finally brought the nurses to Scutari.

As the dauntless Miss Nightingale stepped ashore, followed by her nurses in their ugly brown uniforms and caps, she stood very still for a moment to look the place over. An old Turkish barracks was the principal hospital building. A foul and filthy place it was, and the nurses gasped with dismay as they stared. Then Miss Nightingale stepped forward into the hallway, where wounded and sick men were lying all over the floor. Doctors were not friendly to these "upstart women" invading a man's world, and officers were curt.

The nurses were given a room too small for them, but they did not complain. They had no time, for Miss Nightingale was already ordering things done and persuading the doctors and officers to get them done. She asked for a crew of two hundred convalescent men to scrub floors, and she got them. She then hired their wives to wash dirty linen and clothing. She also reorganized the kitchens, with the help of her friends, Mr. and Mrs. Bracebridge, who had come with her. She added a diet kitchen, for soups and gruels, to replace the tough bones, meat, and bread given to desperately sick men. She slept on a cot in the kitchen, when she had time to sleep.

Miss Nightingale's voice was soft and kind, yet it was firm and strict, too. After a while many doctors and officers began to trust and respect and then to like her. Those who resented her

16

TRINITY CATHOLIC SCHOOL LIBRARY
706 EAST BREVARD STREET
TALLAHASSEE, FLORIDA 32303

authority called her "the Bird." But the sick men grew to worship Miss Nightingale. At night when the wind shook the old Turkish barracks and rats scurried in the walls, suffering men would look up to see this lady coming down the long rows of cots to find out how they were. She held a lamp before her, to light their faces. To them she was "The Lady with a Lamp."

Sometimes Florence paused by a window to listen to the surging waters of the straits, and she smiled a little, thinking of the sound of the River Derwent rushing through Lea Hurst meadows. Every night she walked through "our four miles of cots," as she called the hospital. Then she sat down at a kitchen table to write letters.

Florence Nightingale was becoming a heroine not only to the English, but to everybody, everywhere. She received hundreds of letters a week, often containing money for her work, and she tried to answer them all.

There were three smaller hospitals nearby, and Miss Nightingale undertook to get them all in order. Behind them was the ancient Turkish cemetery. She sighed as she saw how large an English graveyard was growing near it.

In the following spring Miss Nightingale went on shipboard and journeyed to the Crimea itself, to do what she could for the hospitals. The battle of Balaclava had taken its toll of British wounded. This was the engagement in which the charge of the Light Brigade took place, made world-famous later by Tennyson's poem about it. Hospitals were so crowded that men lay in tents pitched all around the harbor. Fever was raging, too. Miss Nightingale was accompanied by Mr. Bracebridge, whose wife

18

was left in charge at Scutari while they were away. The party also included the chef and Tommy, a drummer boy who was a favorite of Miss Nightingale's.

One day the troops in the front lines looked up to see Miss Nightingale riding out to visit them. She was a good horsewoman, and as she passed the Three Mortar Battery the men broke into cheers. Many were soldiers returned to duty from her hospital.

Then Miss Nightingale fell ill with fever and came close to dying. When the news reached England, even Queen Victoria joined in prayers for her recovery. The whole world rejoiced when the crisis passed and she was better. Doctors urged her to return to England, but she refused. She said that she felt like part of the British army, and if they could suffer and endure, then so could she.

When she returned to Scutari, Miss Nightingale decided that the convalescent soldiers should learn to read. "Flo is trying to educate the British army," said Parthenope tartly. At that time soldiers were thought to be closer to brutes than to human beings. There was much talk of not pampering or spoiling them. To Florence Nightingale every man, rich or poor, was a valuable life. Many of these soldiers remembered that she always stood beside the operation table, with her hands quietly folded, suffering with them as they endured operations without ether or chloroform.

Work grew more difficult. Some nurses were dissatisfied and left. Others came when she had not asked for them, and there was no place to put them. Some officers wrote false reports about her, and they were printed in England. When the war ended, in 1856, she returned with a record of hospital work well done. She had also made improvements in the living conditions of the wives who went with the soldiers, as well as for the troops themselves.

When Florence Nightingale returned to England, she was afraid of the grand celebrations prepared to greet her. She left the ship secretly and walked in on her family at Lea Hurst unannounced. Big meetings were held in her honor, nevertheless, and with the money collected at them Florence was able to begin her plans for army hospital reform. She was not well and, as months passed, she did not improve. In spite of this, she intended to carry out her plans. Her next move was to a house in London, where she spent the rest of her life. Parthe had married Lord Verney, a widower with two children, and Florence became a devoted aunt as well as sister.

At the age of thirty-eight, heroic Miss Nightingale became

an invalid. She seldom went out, but spent most of her time on a bed or couch. There she did more hard work than three ordinary people in good health could accomplish. Her friends included government officials, who helped her with her schemes. She worked tirelessly to get better hospitals, better barracks for soldiers, and sanitation reforms in the British colony of India. She also wrote a great deal and saw many people. Everyone thought that she did not have long to live.

During the Civil War in the United States Miss Nightingale gave advice on nursing training and on hospitals, at the request of the American government. She answered thousands of letters, and she directed her household as a general runs an army. Gradually she lost her fragile looks and became a stout old lady who looked rather like Queen Victoria. Yet no visitor who ever came to talk with her left without feeling the great beauty, kindness, and brilliance of her mind and character.

Nursing continued to be her greatest interest. Miss Nightingale directed the training of hospital nurses. In that she ruled with a strict hand. The young nurses must live like nuns, devoted only to their duty. They had to keep diaries, which she read regularly. When they went out on the street, they had to go "by twos." One of them remarked later, with a laugh, that of course they always separated at the corner!

A visit to the "Chief" was an event for a nurse. The young girl walked in shyly, to find Miss Nightingale lying on her couch in her fine black silk dress, with a piece of costly hand-made lace tied over her head. Beside her were pencils and papers, reports, and learned books. At once Miss Nightingale put the nurse at ease, with great charm, and before the girl realized what had happened her shyness had disappeared and she was talking. Then tea and cakes were served, and a cake was given the guest to take home.

Miss Nightingale lived to be ninety years old. She lived so long that she became a legend in her own lifetime. After a while people did not know whether she was really still alive or was only a great memory. Those who actually knew her could have remarked, however, that few living people had such a record of accomplishment.

Queen Victoria herself was not more regal than Miss Nightingale. She is remembered as the great lady who loved people enough to help them by giving her talents, her time, and her strength. She is remembered as a woman walking wearily, yet patiently, through dark rooms, holding up a lighted lamp to see the face of suffering she had come to help.

22

# Kamiano

## FATHER DAMIEN

The little village of Tremeloo, Belgium, in the midst of prosperous farms, was a safe place for the child, Joseph de Veuster, to be born. Windmill sails slowly turned in the brown fields on a cold January day in 1840, when all of the de Veusters came to welcome the new baby. The warm thatched farmhouse was filled with visitors, and with the five older children. In the big kitchen Francois de Veuster thanked his relatives for their good wishes, as he stretched his feet toward the fire and smoked his pipe.

"This Joseph!" roared the baby's godfather, slapping his hand down on the scrubbed table. "He will be a soldier, as I was."

Francois nodded, murmuring, "Perhaps."

"He will be a priest," declared the godmother, "for a priest we must have in the family."

Francois nodded again, "Perhaps. Who knows?"

In Tremeloo the farming people all spoke Flemish, for this was in the northern part of Belgium. They looked down on those who lived in the south, and called them Walloons. So young Joseph spoke Flemish as he grew up, running through the fields after his father and brothers and sisters as they planted and harvested. No one knew yet what he would become — not even he. And he played with the other boys, often getting into trouble in the village for the mischief that he thought up. Sometimes he came home with a nose bloodied by fighting, and was sternly punished by his father.

When he was older, Joseph wandered along the River Laak, watching his flock of sheep. He flung himself into the grass as the flock grazed and fixed his eyes on the sky, wondering whether it would look the same in faraway lands.

His favorite time of day was late afternoon, when his mother, with her kettles bubbling and her bread baking, called the three younger children to her. As they sat on stools beside her, she told them stories of the saints and martyrs of their Catholic church, and of the ancient days of Rome. The three youngest de Veusters, Auguste, Pauline, and Joseph, admired both the saints and the soldiers. They played games in which they were knights of the Crusade, or Christian martyrs torn by Roman lions.

The older children of the family were to be farmers, and help their father, while these younger ones would have a choice of other occupations — with their father's approval, of course.

Auguste became quieter as he grew taller, and when he told his father and mother that he meant to be a priest, no one was surprised. Then Pauline decided to become a nun.

"Well and good," said Father Francois, smoking his pipe after supper beside the fire. "And Joseph shall be a merchant."

Joseph, who did not know what he wanted, had no idea of questioning this. Father's word was law in the family. Joseph

26

went fishing and hunting with other boys, and he also liked to help the blacksmith in the village. The blacksmith was glad of his help, for he saw that this boy was very strong and very skillful with tools. Yet Joseph had fits of moodiness, when he didn't like to be with his friends. At such times he went to the river and stretched out on the ground to watch the clouds drift overhead.

From time to time he still got into trouble through fighting, as his hot temper rose. Joseph was never a real scholar, as Auguste was, but he agreed readily enough when his father offered to send him to a business school in the Walloon part of Belgium. He fought the boys who made fun of his country clothes and Flemish speech, and proved so handy with his fists that they let him alone. He made no friends, and became silent and moody, but he did not complain. In his letters home, he said that he was making progress in his studies and learning the

27

French language as fast as he possibly could.

Joseph was very lonely, however, and he did not like his work. He looked anxiously for letters from Auguste, now in a monastery of the Sacred Heart in Louvain. Joseph was nineteen, and was a strong, handsome youth, when he decided that his life, too, must be given to the church. For some time he put off telling his father of this. Then, at last, he sat down and wrote a letter explaining his reasons for wishing to enter the priesthood.

One day a carriage drove up to the school, and the old farmer got down, pipe in mouth. When Joseph came out, in some surprise, his father told him to pack his things, for he was to visit his brother in the monastery. As they rolled along, Joseph heard news of the family, and of Pauline, who had just taken final vows and become a nun. After that they said little to each other, but when Joseph got out at the monastery, he knew that his father meant him to stay there. As he turned toward the gate he saw his brother standing inside, a smile of welcome on his face.

At first Joseph spent his time working on an addition to the buildings. He had to study hard, too, for he must learn Latin as well as church subjects. He was a young man who talked little, and the workmen laying bricks with him were surprised to find that he was as good at the trade as they were. When Joseph heard the men talking about the shaky smoke stack that they had to remove to make way for a new chapel, he offered to climb up and take it down. This was a dangerous job, and the men almost held their breath as Joseph climbed carefully to the top and began to remove the bricks.

"He'll be killed. What a fool!"

Joseph worked slowly and skillfully and brought the smoke stack down, brick by brick. Although it tottered dangerously, it did not fall with him. From that day the workmen respected the new brother in spite of his silent ways.

As his studies increased, Joseph had difficulty. He was never much of a scholar, and for some time his brother, whose monastery name was now Pamphile, had to help him with classical and church lessons. This was far harder for Joseph than tearing down a chimney. When the time came to choose his own monastery name, he took the name of Damien. Damien had been a physician, saint, and martyr of the fourth century.

The following year Damien was sent to Paris to finish his studies. It was here that he heard, for the first time, of the missionary work in the South Seas. Damien wrote to Pamphile that nothing in life would please him so much as going to work among the natives of the Sandwich Islands. Pamphile wrote back that he shared this wish, and the brothers began to hope that they might go together. When he returned to Belgium, Damien and Pamphile went to lectures in the monastery school, and made plans. They would hope, when Damien was ordained, to be sent out to work in the islands with other missionary priests.

One day Damien heard the monks talking excitedly. They were saying that a group of brothers was to be sent to the far Pacific Islands. Pamphile's name was on the list. Damien almost ran as he went to find out about his own. It was not there, for Damien was not yet ordained. As the group was preparing to sail, an epidemic of typhus fever broke out, and Pamphile became seriously ill. Damien nursed him night and day and was thankful to see his brother recover when so many had died.

One day Pamphile, weak and pale, smiled at Damien.

"Brother," he said quietly, "you wished to go more than I. I am not fit for a long sea voyage, and the time to sail is drawing near. Why don't you write to the superior of our order and ask him to send you instead?"

The superior gave his consent, and Damien started on the long voyage to the islands called Sandwich, later to be known as the Hawaiian Islands. With him were nine other priests and a group of nuns, all going to Honolulu. The ship sailed from the port of Bremerhaven, Germany, to the sounds of creaking timbers, cheers from the crowd on shore, and outward-bound sea chanteys roared by the sailors.

The voyage was long, and at first waves rolled the little ship about until all of the passengers except Damien went to their bunks and stayed there for days. Father Damien was never sick, as he walked the decks or argued about religion with Captain Gerken, who was a Protestant.

Then the waters of the south Atlantic became calm and warm, and even the pale nuns climbed to the decks for fresh

air. Soon they sailed around Cape Horn, where storms tossed the ship like a chip on huge seas. At last the vessel moved into the Pacific Ocean, and after four months on board passengers saw green-topped palms glistening on the beautiful island of Oahu.

Father Damien leaned over the rail to watch a swarm of brown men push out from shore in their outrigger canoes, heading for the ship. The canoes carried pineapples, bananas, and other tropical fruits strange to the newcomers. Natives climbed to the decks with garlands of flowers in their hands, and some leaped into the clear waters to swim about like tawny fish.

Father Damien and his fellow passengers went ashore in Honolulu to walk through streets where blossoms of purple, yellow, and red hung over thatched roofs of houses. What a different world from that of Tremeloo! Yet, for some strange reason that he could not name, Damien felt that his whole life was meant to be lived in these islands.

As Father Damien looked curiously about him, he remembered all of the things that he had heard about the islands. For many years sailors returning to Europe had described them as

31

a paradise. When Captain Cook had arrived there in 1778, these handsome brown people had been carefree and happy. Then with white men came several diseases never known in the islands before, and the people, living in the midst of beauty, suffered terribly from sickness.

Damien's first parish was in the Puno district on the island of Hawaii. Hawaii is the largest of the eight inhabited islands of the group, which lies two thousand miles from the western shores of America. He went there on a small steamer and found, on landing, that he was the only white man in his parish. He could look up to the high peaks of volcanoes, and when he walked, his feet trod on lava stone, poured out of the fiery volcanoes in some dim past.

The new priest looked about him. Natives lived in small huts, where they had little work to do. Fruits were easy to pick from coconut, breadfruit, and banana trees, and fish could always be caught in the bright waters. Father Damien was not an idle man, and he set about building immediately. First the parish must have a good chapel. Then the buildings of the natives must be improved. There should be a school. There was much to do—and no time should be lost. The hardest task that he had was to make the smiling, good-natured men of Puno work. They did not understand why they should.

Father Damien kept at his task with an energy that never left him, in spite of the tropical warmth of the islands.

"Come, we must cut trees. We must have better buildings. We must have a good water supply."

He shouted, urged, and commanded. The natives called

him Kamiano, a name chosen from the Hawaiian language. They respected him, even though they shrugged when he shouted, and in their soft voices asked "Why?"

Cool breezes carried music sung by men and women as they swayed in their old dances. The white beach was bright with their colored skirts and shirts, and with their laughter as they brought in a load of shining fish. Then among the strong and smiling young men and women Father Damien began to notice some who were sick and deformed in the horrible way that meant leprosy. This disease was one of those brought to the islands by white men from Europe. In the Middle Ages in European countries lepers had been forced to wear gowns with hoods and to ring bells to warn healthy people not to come near them. Here they were supposed to be sent to a hospital in Honolulu. When the hospital had become overcrowded, the king of the islands ordered all lepers to go to an uninhabited island called Molokai. This became known as the land of the "living dead."

Father Damien watched silently as sick men, women, and children were taken from their families and sent to Molokai. Night after night he walked up and down the moonlit beach, thinking of it. Then he went to Honolulu and told his bishop that he wanted to go to live on Molokai.

He sailed at once, with a shipload of lepers who were in the early stages of this slow disease, and his bishop made the trip with him. Early one morning, as dawn crept up the sky, Father Damien and the bishop landed from a small boat, the first of those bringing lepers in from the anchored ship. Behind the cove where the lepers lived, they saw high mountain crags. As they walked

34

slowly toward the village, frightfully crippled people hobbled out of broken-down huts to meet them.

The bishop spoke to them, telling them that Father Damien, their Kamiano, had come to live with them. Damien saw that they did not understand how a healthy man could come there to live, and that they distrusted him. He knew that he must show them that he was not afraid. When the bishop had sailed away, Father Damien went to sleep under a big pandanus tree. Next morning he rose at dawn, inspected the dirty huts, and made his plans.

No one could look on a leper without horror, for the disease was so terrible that it slowly changed the body, and caused the face to have an expression known as "the lion look." Father Damien called together all of the men who were not too ill to work. He explained that he wanted them to have a clean, decent

35

village, and not to live like wild animals any longer.

As weeks passed, Kamiano tore down huts and put up new ones. He taught men and women to plant gardens. He went every day into huts to care for the sick. He saw that the village must have fresh water, for people had to walk such long distances into the mountains for it that they could not get enough to keep clean.

When the leper ship returned, Father Damien went back to Honolulu to talk to the bishop. He had some money given him to buy water pipes, which he took back to Molokai, and then organized a work crew to bring water to the village. Every night for weeks he slept under his pandanus tree. It was not until all of the other huts were built that he made one for himself. He conducted masses in his little chapel, and went to Honolulu less often, for he saw that he was avoided by healthy people, as if he had the disease himself, and he preferred to be with the sick.

There was trouble constantly because the Board of Health did not want to give money to the leper colony for food, tools, and medical supplies. Kamiano became gruff and rougher in his ways, but he was always kind to the sick. On Molokai the village changed, and everything improved under the care of Father Damien.

One day Molokai celebrated the greatest event ever known there. Every man, woman, and child who could walk or crawl came to the beach to watch a ship drop anchor. The lepers were dressed in bright cotton clothing, and they carried garlands of flowers. Father Damien had trained a little band of musicians who played their simple instruments. As a small boat came in to

36

the beach, music filled the air, and children advanced before an arch of flowers to greet their royal guest. Princess Liliuokalani, who had heard with great interest of the work of Father Damien, had come to visit the colony.

The princess spent the day on Molokai, looking with pity on her suffering people and seeing the conditions under which they lived. When she returned to Honolulu, she sent to Father Damien a letter of praise for his work, and with it the jeweled insignia of the Royal Order of Kalahua. Newspapers printed the story, and from that time on Father Damien of Molokai was famous throughout the world. A group of capable nurses who were nuns was sent to help in his hospital, and distinguished visitors arrived from time to time. With this new help Father Damien was able to start an orphanage for sick children.

For some years it looked as if Kamiano led a charmed life.

Although he shared his food and even his pipe with the lepers, he was always well and vigorous. Then, one day, his congregation saw him step into his pulpit in chapel, and heard his calm voice saying, "We lepers—" The doctors and nurses who came there knew that they did not need to catch leprosy, if they were careful. But Damien, who had come alone to live in a colony of outcasts, had gained their confidence by not showing fear, and had deliberately given his life to them.

When he died in the terrible way that lepers die, in April, 1889, many things were printed about him. Some reported that Father Damien was rude and rough and unclean, and that he was given to ordering people around too much. Robert Louis Stevenson, called Tusitala, or the Story Teller, by the natives, lived in the islands, where he hoped to recover from tuberculosis. He went to Molokai to learn the truth about Father Damien. When he returned he wrote a famous letter telling of the great work and sacrifice of the priest.

Father Damien of Molokai is honored by Hawaiians and by the world. His work there brought the pitiful conditions of outcast people to public attention, and opened the way to assistance for them. Medical research, care, and understanding have greatly reduced the number of the "living dead," since Kamiano first set foot on Molokai to show others that every life is worth helping.

# Plant Wizard

GEORGE WASHINGTON CARVER

A little boy plodded slowly along a lonely road in Missouri, in the summer of 1874. Over his shoulder swung his belongings, tied in an old shawl, fastened to a stick. He was small and thin, and he did not talk much, for his voice was only a piping squeak. Yet his large eyes moved from side to side and he saw more than most other people did. As his bare feet moved in the dust, the boy felt his shoes bounce against his chest. New shoes should not be ruined by wear, so he had hung them around his neck by the laces. He was tired and rather hungry, but he smiled as he felt the sun and the breeze on his face. Birds sang, all trees were his friends, and every clump of grass and wild flower seemed to nod to him.

This was George Washington Carver, setting out to seek his fortune. It was astonishing that such a small Negro boy should start out alone to the town of Neosho to learn to read and write; yet it was even more surprising that he was alive at all. Many times he had heard his good foster mother tell him of a dreadful night during the Civil War. George was a tiny baby then. He did not remember how his sister had been killed, how his older brother had escaped and hidden, and how he and his mother had

41

been stolen by slave raiders. These slaves belonged to a German farmer and his wife named Carver who were fond of them. Carver had ridden out in pursuit of the thieves and had found tiny, sickly George abandoned by the roadside. His mother had never been heard of again. Carver had given a good horse to the neighbor who had helped him in the search. Sometimes George looked down at his own spindly legs and wondered if he was worth as much as a horse. There was some doubt about it in his mind.

After a few years George's brother, Jim, went away, and George did not see him again. George was not strong enough to do farm work, so Frau Carver taught him to cook and wash clothes. He taught himself about trees and plants, for he loved all growing things. When George was no taller than the highest weed on the roadside, he made the Carver garden the finest in the neighborhood.

A farmer friend of the Carvers saw how bright he was, and said that he ought to be taught to read. This farmer gave George a book on plants. Although George did not want to leave the Carvers, and they hated to see him go, he knew that he must learn to read. Now George had a dollar in his pocket to pay for his schooling. As for food and shelter — well, he could work hard. He was on his way to the nearest school for Negroes.

George reached Neosho by nightfall and crept into an old barn to sleep in the hay. Next morning he found the one-room school and paid his dollar to enter. For several weeks George slept in the barn beside a stray dog. He earned his food by washing dishes or cutting wood. Then, early one morning, the man who owned the barn came in and saw the little boy curled up beside

the dog, and almost hidden under a mound of hay.

"Well, now, what are you doing in my barn?"

George jumped up in a fright, and found it impossible to speak. The young man smiled and said, "You look hungry, boy. Come in the house."

Inside the warm kitchen a young wife was frying bacon and eggs and baking corn bread. She gave George some hot food, and then the Martins sat down to hear his story. When he finished, speaking slowly and politely in his squeaky voice, they looked at each other, nodded, and offered him the shed to sleep in. George stayed there for some months and did odd jobs for the young couple. As he sat in the kitchen in the evenings he heard them talk of the West and of how they might join one of the wagon trains rolling through Missouri. He was not surprised when they decided to go. The day that they left, George sat down on the steps and wondered what he was going to do now.

He heard a voice. "Boy, get your things and come with me."

George looked up. There stood Aunt Mariah, an elderly Negro woman whom he knew in the town. He jumped up, collected his few clothes and the food left him by the Martins, and

43

went to her little house, where he soon felt very much at home.

George lived with Aunt Mariah and Uncle Andy until he was thirteen and had learned far more than his teacher in the school knew. As soon as he could read, he borrowed every book that he could find and remembered all that he read. The day came when he knew that, to learn more, he must start out alone on the road again. Saying good-by to his friends was hard. He was fortunate in making friends, but always seemed to have to leave them.

George went to Fort Scott, Kansas. There he got work in a hotel and was allowed to sleep on a cot on the back porch. He went to school and found that, even here, he knew more about plants than did the teacher. Since George had very little time to go out into the country, he began to draw trees and flowers. He also got a little paint box, and painted flowers. He joined the art class of his school, and soon became known for his pictures. When he had again learned all that the school could teach him, George was on his way once more. He had grown tall and much stronger, and now his voice was strong, too, though as soft and gentle as ever. He had to earn his living, so he signed up as a laborer on the new railroad that was being built across the western plains, and became a camp cook for a while. Then later, he worked picking fruit or on ranches. Finally he went to Olathe, Kansas, to go to school again.

Here George made more good friends, for everybody liked him. He lived with a Negro couple whom he called Aunt Lucy and Uncle Seymour, and finished high school. Then he went back to visit the Carvers, who urged him to stay with them and farm their land. George was tempted, but somehow he knew that

44

he must do something more. He wanted more learning. He wanted
to go to college.

"College?" asked Frau Carver, folding her hands beneath her
big white apron. "*Ja,* you should go to college. But how can you?"

George smiled, and nodded. He meant to try. First he ap-
plied to Highland College, in Kansas, but was turned down because he was a Negro. Discouraged, he homesteaded land and
tried to make a farm of his own for a while, but the earth was very
poor, and he gave it up. One day he wandered into a church in
Winterset, Iowa, and joined in singing a hymn. As his rich voice
rolled forth, the minister noticed him. Next day Parson Milholland
looked George up and invited him to his home. Mrs. Milholland
was a musician and was so interested in this talented young man
that she gave him music lessons. Mr. Milholland said that he
would locate a college that would take George. Simpson College,

45

in Iowa, accepted him, and so once again George set out, this time to enter art school.

Making a living was always a problem, but it was not a new one to George Carver. He found a shed, got permission to use it, and started a laundry service for other students. During his second year there, as George pushed the hot iron expertly back and forth over shirts, his thoughts were busy with his future. What did he want to do? He liked painting, but he realized now that he did not want to spend all of his time as an artist. Science interested him far more.

The following year George disappointed his art teacher by leaving Simpson College to go to the Iowa State College in Ames, to study agriculture and botany. And so, at twenty-seven years of age, the tall, gentle Negro began the study of plant life. He was soon known as a remarkable student, and he made many friends. George Carver began to draw attention by his work with plants. After he had been at the State College a few years he was called a "plant wizard," for his long fingers could do more than anyone thought possible. He worked day and night, waiting on table, doing anything to make a simple living. But his happiest hours were spent in the greenhouses with plants and flowers.

George Washington Carver received his degree in 1894, and was asked to teach at the college. Now he could smile when he remembered that he had once wondered whether he was worth as much as a horse! Here, in Ames, Iowa, he had great laboratories to work in and every opportunity to do the things that he could do so well. After a few years George had earned another degree, and was happy in his teaching. It really looked as if this was his

46

place on earth, and his wanderings were over.

Then, one day, up from Alabama came a Negro man whose name was also Washington. This was Booker T. Washington, an educator who was spending his life trying to improve education for his own race. At the end of the Civil War Negroes were free, but most of them were unable to read and write. Many small schools were started for them, but money was scarce, and people had hardly enough to support themselves. Booker T. Washington had bought a piece of washed-out earth in Alabama. Here he had taught a few young men to build a schoolhouse. They built it of bricks that they made themselves from the red clay of the land.

Carver sat quietly and listened as Washington talked to him about the beginning of the school at Tuskegee. He said little, but he nodded every now and then, and sometimes frowned. Washington spoke of the Negro farmers and their wives and children. They had cotton fields and a few other small crops, but could never grow enough both to feed themselves and to sell a surplus to get cash for clothing and supplies. A man who understood farming was desperately needed to teach young men and women to get better crops from their land.

Dr. Carver listened carefully to the big dark man who talked so earnestly about the needs of the Negro people. He made his decision. Quietly, and with a smile, he told Booker Washington that he would come to Tuskegee to do all that he could. This "plant wizard," with such a brilliant future ahead of him at a fine university, would go to live in the poverty-stricken Negro country in Alabama.

Not long after, as he stood and saw the Tuskegee school for the first time, Dr. Carver wondered how he could accomplish anything here at all. The brick building was surrounded by fields overgrown with weeds, washed into gullies by rains. Inside the school he found no laboratory and nothing with which to work. But George Washington Carver had not been a professor all of his busy years. He had worked with hot irons, wash tubs, cookstoves, the ax, the hoe, and the plow. In his classes he had only a few young men, with little education and no knowledge beyond the cotton fields. But they knew poverty as well as he did, and they could be trained to make much of very little. He proposed that he help them make their own laboratory.

He led them on expeditions to the dump heaps around the nearest towns. This was a search that became a treasure hunt. The students went through trash piles in alleys, and asked housewives for broken pans, lamps, and kettles. When they had collected a great pile of cast-off utensils, Professor Carver showed them pictures that he had drawn of laboratory equipment. Long hours the boys worked with broken articles — cleaning, mending, making new things from old ones.

And then Dr. Carver got a two-horse plow and went to work

himself. Straight furrows stretched out behind him, and students who had thought of farming as ignorant work, not fit for the educated, felt ashamed. Dr. Carver sent them for bucket after bucket of black muck and leaf mold from swamps and woods, and manure from the barns. Then he planted cowpeas! Everybody gasped. Who ever heard of such a thing? Cowpeas were good only for pigs. Cotton was the cash money crop. When the peas were picked, this strange teacher cooked them, and they were so delicious that the students couldn't eat enough.

After that, Dr. Carver planted sweet potatoes, and the earth yielded eighty bushels to the acre. This was unheard of in that country, and now the boys who had not wanted to farm began to speak of being "agriculturists." After a few years of these crops Dr. Carver planted cotton in the enriched fields and showed that crop rotation could help the soil.

Nothing on earth was wasted. That was the belief of this man who seemed to have magic in his fingers. Every day he had a whole handful of new ideas, too. He searched the woods and fields and brought home plants, leaves, and roots. Then he took them to his laboratory and made them into useful products, or medicines, or food. He told his students that they must learn to "see." They must always see something good in nature. They must always look for something that would benefit mankind.

Not even a few handfuls of dirt were too humble to interest Dr. Carver. Yet he wanted almost nothing for himself. He wore old clothes and ancient shoes, and he ate the food prepared for students. He required no luxuries of any kind. His love for flowers was with him, as it had been since he could remember.

Instead of painting flowers, Dr. Carver grew them, and he was never seen without a blossom on his coat.

One day the professor's foot slipped as he wandered through a swamp, and he fell into the mud. When he stood up, he saw with surprise that the mud on his hands was blue. He stared at it and then smiled in delight. He brought a pail, collected some mud, and took it back to the school. Not long after that, Dr. Carver told his class that here they had good paint all around them — and had never known it. When the white farmers of a nearby town asked him to speak, Dr. Carver discovered that their new little church was unpainted because of the cost. A few days later he appeared with some students and several buckets of blue paint. The church was soon covered with a handsome blue coating, and the paint stood up in all weathers.

Far and wide people talked about this gentle, hard-working

51

scientist, who could make something out of nothing. His fame spread, and strangers came to see him. The school began to grow, and more students came to it. Yet, as always, money was the problem. Booker T. Washington was often out trying to raise money, lecturing and explaining the needs. Dr. Carver could think of only one way that he could make money for the school. He could play the piano as well as he could paint. A concert tour was arranged, and money came in for new equipment and supplies for the laboratories of Dr. Carver.

There was something else that interested the scientist. He asked himself: How can I reach the poor farmer who needs help, and cannot come to Tuskegee? A thought struck him: If he cannot come here, why can't I go to him?

A wagon was fitted out, and a program arranged. Dr. Carver made talks on crop rotation, on chicken raising, on the difficult problems of the farmers. This was the first movable school for agriculture, and the first demonstration wagon to go out to the people. Farmers' wives were told how to make good pickles and preserves and how to can food well. There was not a single subject that Dr. Carver didn't know, and not one activity that he couldn't actually do himself. Later on, the wagon carried new types of plows and garden tools. And, at one time, the demonstration collection included a live cow.

Farmers as well as students were learning from Tuskegee. Slowly money came in, and Dr. Carver was offered a larger salary. He heard the offer with a smile, and asked, "What will I do with more money?"

He had no interest in money for himself, but his interest in

the land and its products grew stronger every year. When the boll weevil, "that little black bug," as the song says, came eastward from Mexico and Texas, Dr. Carver saw the danger in advance. This bug could destroy the very plants of the cotton completely and quickly. He begged farmers to stop planting cotton that year and to plow cotton stalks under to make a belt to stop the weevil. Not understanding, they refused. Dr. Carver urged farmers to spray their cotton fields with poison, and then to plant peanuts. But they refused again, and the boll weevil took over. When the cotton was destroyed, farmers were willing to plant peanuts. But then, because the peanut crop was so large, prices went down.

Dr. Carver set to work in his laboratory. He paid no attention to the things said against him for giving such advice. For many weeks he worked far into the night, and when he called people in to see the results, he showed them cheese, milk, and almost two dozen other products made from the peanut. Later he made other things: face powder, printer's ink, soaps, vinegar, creosote, butter, dyes, and many more. He experimented in the same way with the common sweet potato. Now the farmers had a market for peanuts —and the scientific world was excited. Synthetic products could be valuable. Big business was interested in the fact that useful products could be made from so many things that were formerly thrown out as useless waste.

Dr. Carver was the great pioneer in this field. When Booker T. Washington died, the scientist was offered positions with high salaries at other colleges and in manufacturing plants. He chose to stay at Tuskegee because his interest in helping the poor farmer was as strong as ever. He spent more hours in his laboratory and did less teaching, and in his spare time he painted flowers, worked with them in the greenhouses, played the piano, or made fine tapestries.

When visitors came and asked, "Is that the famous Dr. Carver?" the students thought it a good joke to say, "Yes, and he is still wearing the same suit that he had on when he came to Tuskegee."

Before Dr. Carver died in 1943, he was happy to see a fine new laboratory set up there under his direction. Now he knew that the students could go on to more knowledge under other teachers. He had taught them to see more than others saw, as he did, and he tried to teach them to listen well also. He refused to be discouraged because he was a Negro. George Washington Carver was a man who never looked down on any kind of hard work, and he was one who used his genius to help the people of his own race—those who had so little opportunity. His own love of all things that grow made the work of Dr. Carver an important part of the lives of all people, of all races.

54

# Good Neighbor

## JANE ADDAMS

A little girl stood frowning down at her hands, turning her right thumb around to look at it. She wished that she could see that it was flattening out into a real "miller's thumb," the kind that came from constant rubbing of the wheat between thumb and finger.

She reached into a pile of wheat and slowly rubbed it. Then she turned her hands over and scowled at the backs of them. Why couldn't she have those tiny red and blue marks that millers had? Father still had them on his hands, and he had a miller's thumb, too, even though he was now the owner of the mill instead of a worker. She asked the miller about it. He only laughed at her, and when he ground the millstones and sparks hit his hands and made the tiny red marks, he teased her about wanting to be a miller.

The mill stood among tall elms at the edge of Cedarville in northwestern Illinois. Jane had been born in 1860 in the big house nearby. In the years since the Civil War her father had become the most important man of the village, for he was wise and thoughtful, as well as a good businessman. He was a Quaker. He had been in the legislature along with Abraham Lincoln. Jane was proud

57

of the fact that her father had letters from the martyred president, letters which began jokingly: "My Dear Mr. Double-D Addams."

Near the flour mill was a sawmill, and the Addams children had a wonderful place to play along the little stream that turned the wheel of the flour mill. Jane, who was the youngest, had a spinal curvature that caused her to walk with her toes turned in, and with her head slightly to one side. Her mother had died when she was a baby, so Jane had given all of her love and admiration to her handsome father. The other children—Mary, Martha, Weber, and Alice—were much older. Nurse Polly, who had come west with them, was a part of the family also.

Jane was a rather silent girl, playing alone in the mill and under the trees, with kittens and dogs for companions. Secretly she felt that her father should have had a beautiful daughter, and she tried not to walk beside him in town, since she did not want strangers to know that a fine-looking man had such a homely little girl.

One day, when she drove through town with him, Jane noticed that the laborers lived in poor and ugly houses. She asked her father why this was so. He tried to explain to her that not every child was as fortunate as she.

Jane said thoughtfully, "When I grow up I will live in a beautiful big house, as I do now, but it will be with ugly little houses around it, and I will invite all of the other children to play in my nice yard."

John Addams looked down at the serious face and smiled. He wondered sadly how her health would be as she grew older.

Jane read a great deal in her father's books, for he had a larger

library than most in the village. She wanted to understand the books that her father read, and she tried to understand, also, his concern for others. She began to have a strange dream, one that came back to her from time to time for some years. She dreamed that she was alone on earth and that all by herself, somehow, she had to make a wagon wheel. She knew that the future of the world depended on it. Jane always woke up from this dream terrified, and as soon as she could, she went to the village to watch the blacksmith at work. Perhaps she could learn how.

When Jane was about eight, her father married a widow who had two sons. This event started a happier life for Jane, for one of the boys was about her age and now she had a playmate. They played that they were Crusaders on the way to the Holy Land, and sometimes these games continued from day to day for weeks.

When Jane was seventeen, she entered a college called Rockford Seminary, which was not far from her home town. She was bitterly disappointed because her father wished to keep her close to home and refused to allow her to go East to Smith College.

Yet, after a while, she made friends and began to enjoy the life of the school. The girls at Rockford Seminary were serious and studious, and they had such strong religious beliefs that many of them later went into missionary work. Jane, although she was rather religious, refused to become a missionary. Like her father, she made her own decisions and was not swayed by what others did.

When she was graduated from Rockford Seminary, she entered the Women's Medical College of Philadelphia. Then her spinal trouble grew worse, until she had to have an operation and spend some months in bed at the home of a married sister. When Jane was up and well again, she realized sadly that she could not study anything so strenuous as medicine. What was she to do? Her family thought that travel would be good for Jane, so she went to Europe for two years. To her Europe was a world of lovely landscapes, fine pictures, concerts, and beautiful old buildings. Jane enjoyed them all. Yet there was a different scene that she remembered above all others.

One Saturday night she joined a group of sight-seers on a horse-drawn bus in London. The bus rattled into the worst slum in the sprawling city. Jane, who was sitting on top, could look down on a picture that was like a horrible nightmare. By the light of two flaring gas lamps ragged men, women, and children pushed and fought to buy vegetables and fruit left over from the week's sales. For halfpennies they got rotten cabbages and potatoes, and devoured them, skin and all. All of her life Jane Addams remembered the sight of clawlike hands raised to bid for decaying vegetables.

After that, she visited slums wherever she went in Europe, returning to her own country with more knowledge of social conditions than most travelers ever get. Her health was quite good now, and she was twenty-seven years old. What was she to do? After a time she joined a friend, Ellen Starr, and returned to Europe for another trip. One day in London Jane declared that she was tired of a useless life. Ellen replied thoughtfully that she felt the same. Custom did not permit women of their position to go out to work, except to teach. Ellen was already a teacher, but she and Jane wanted to do something more. They decided to visit Toynbee Hall, in London's East End slums. Perhaps they could get an idea.

Toynbee Hall was the world's first settlement house. As Jane and Ellen walked through it, and saw the friendly people who were trying to make this a clubhouse for the neighborhood, they looked at each other and smiled. It was not a "mission" run by a church, but was simply a place where people could come together for classes, clubs, and social life. Suddenly Jane thought: This is a big house in the midst of little ones! This is the kind of house that I have wanted—one that I can share with my neighbors.

That night Jane and Ellen talked late, and plans were made. They returned to America and at once began to put their plans into action. After a visit to her sisters, Jane studied bookkeeping, for her "Big House" must be well run. Ellen had no extra money to put into it, but Jane did have some left to her by her father, who had died several years before. She went to Chicago to find her home among the poor, in a district to which most of her friends never came.

Chicago, in the eighteen-eighties, was a spreading, growing city, where people poured in from the East, by every train, wagon, and ship. As she walked about, Jane thought that this place was like a great overgrown boy, shooting up so fast that he could not tell what to do with his feet and hands. In one part of Chicago the rich lived in big mansions on fashionable avenues, and seemed unaware of the vast slums.

All around Jane in the dirty streets swarmed men, women, and children from every country in Europe, shouting and talking in every kind of language. Many could not speak English at all. They crowded into tenements and into noisy, dark factories and big cattle stockyards where they worked. They all wanted to be Americans — but they did not know how. Chicago was really a huge collection of foreign cities flung together without plan.

Halsted Street was called the longest straight street in the world, for it ran thirty-two miles. Jane rode slowly along it in a hired carriage, thinking that these people must be her neighbors and that here she must find her house. Then she saw it! It was a thirty-year-old mansion, formerly the home of the wealthy Hull family, when the street had seen better days. Now it was filled

with little flats, and had a storeroom and saloon on the ground floor.

Jane and Ellen Starr found the owner, Miss Helen Culver, and rented part of the house. They had a promise of getting all of it later, when a lease ran out. A friend, Mary Keyser, came to live and work with them, and Jane brought furniture from her old home in Cedarville. They decided to call it Hull House. It was to be a neighborhood settlement home in the midst of Russians, Germans, Greeks, Poles, Italians, and Irish. The whole neighborhood was dirty, noisy, and filled with the scent of foreign foods.

They had no sooner cleaned the house and moved in than there was a knock at the front door. A young mother asked if they would keep her baby while she went to work that day. When Miss Addams spoke to her in Italian, her face broke into a delighted smile. Next day more babies arrived at the door, and Hull House had a day nursery. As the three residents wondered what to do with all of these children every day, the problem was unexpectedly solved for them. A young girl from a wealthy family arrived at their door to ask if she could help.

"What can you do?" asked Jane.

"I can look after children," she answered with a smile, looking around at the noisy guests.

Jane Addams soon discovered that there were others, men as well as women, who wanted to do something at Hull House. After a few weeks, evening classes for girls and boys were started, and clubs as well as dances and concerts planned. Carpentry, sewing, and music were taught. More and more men and women came shyly in and were overjoyed to talk to Miss Addams in their

64

native tongues. The whole neighborhood buzzed with the knowledge that Jane Addams could speak several languages. Hull House was open to its neighbors, and its neighbors came.

As the three residents planned and worked and organized, they had many problems. "Why," asked Jane Addams, "shouldn't these people from countries where they saw so much art, have some to see here?" She started art classes and put good pictures on the walls of Hull House.

There were no playgrounds in Chicago at that time, and tenement children had to stay in the dirty streets or be locked in cold rooms while their parents worked. Streets where they played were so filthy with refuse that it was difficult to walk in them. Garbage overflowed big wooden boxes placed in the middle of streets.

Early one morning sleepy workmen saw Miss Addams plodding through the ankle-deep refuse. As the sun rose, women hung out of windows to watch. What was the lady doing? She held up her skirts above her shoe tops, out of the dirt, and every now and then she stopped to write something in a notebook. This street was so dirty that it was hard to tell whether it was paved with cobblestones or not. There was a broken pump in a yard here— this she noted down—and a tenement without any pump there. Why were those garbage boxes not emptied? Miss Addams had accepted a job as sanitary inspector for the city, and was seeing that the laws were enforced.

One thing led to another. Jane Addams saw that little could be done unless these people could make higher wages. So she began to study such problems. She tried to get better laws passed, for shorter hours and more wages. She also tried to help get laws to make landlords improve tenements. More than anything else she tried to make those who ran local and national government agencies understand that there must be laws to keep children from working long hours in factories, and to send them to school. Hull House organized the first fresh-air camps for children in Chicago, to send them out of the slums for summer vacations.

People in other places talked of Hull House. Many visitors came to see Hull House at work, but when they arrived it was not always easy to find Miss Addams. She was doing many things. She added speaking engagements to her schedule. She had a simple message. She asked for understanding of these foreign-born people, and concern for their children.

Every day she could see hungry children climbing over garbage boxes. After all, she thought, they are better off than the little ones who work in factories and mills! She remembered her

66

own happy childhood, playing in the dusty flour mill, and the smell of sawdust in the sawmill. She thought of the brook under the trees where she had spent sunny days, and of the blacksmith shop. She remembered the great wheel in her dream. Perhaps she was still trying to make that wheel to roll the world toward a better life. But she was not alone. She had helpers at Hull House. In addition to her friends there, others came from many places. Hull House was becoming famous.

Yet Hull House continued to have problems. On Halsted Street young girls and boys grew up ashamed of their parents because the old folks could not speak English. The older people had Old-World ways and customs and could not understand their American children.

One day Jane was picking her way through the street refuse when she passed a tenement house where an old woman sat with an ancient loom. Miss Addams stopped to watch as the knobby fingers made delicate woven patterns. She had been searching in her thoughts for some way to help younger people understand the values of the older ones.

She went home and proposed a plan for a "labor museum."

67

A room was fitted out with several looms, benches, and embroidery frames. The neighborhood was searched for women who had these skills. They came to Hull House and there made fine laces, weavings, and embroideries. The men did wood carving and other crafts of their native countries. When the museum was running smoothly, the younger people were invited to watch, and they came away with a new respect for their old folk.

As the years passed and the circle of activities at Hull House widened, Miss Addams began to try to put more and more time into studying national laws and improving them. She wrote the story of her life, and other books and articles. She was considered an authority on social conditions, and she worked for world peace. In 1931, Jane Addams received the Nobel Peace Prize, jointly with a friend.

As Hull House grew, the neighborhood around it changed. Instead of Germans, people from Central Europe, Mexicans, and Negroes moved in. Later the Mexican population grew large. Languages changed with changing times. Chicago changed, too. Streets were better and were cleaner, and laws were passed to improve tenements, provide running water, and good sanitary conditions. Children had playgrounds, as well as more fresh air camps, and better education. And child labor laws kept them out of factories, and in school.

When Jane Addams died at the age of seventy-five, Hull House had grown large. Many buildings had been added to it, and many devoted people worked there. Yet it remained the "Big House" among little ones, where Miss Addams had invited her neighbors to come, in brotherhood and friendship.

68

# North to Labrador

## WILFRED GRENFELL

Gray wind-swept clouds scudded across the sky above the coast of England as people ran from their homes, from taverns and fields toward the Sands of Dee. Two boys joined the fisherfolk, dashing out of the gate of the big house on the hill when their watchful nurse was not looking. Overhead gulls circled and turned, with mournful cries. Wilfred and his brother, Algernon, joined the knot of women, who were making little cries that sounded as sad as the gull songs.

Wilfred had to bite his lips to keep from crying **as he** saw the boats pulled in onto the sands and two young fishermen lifted out. An old doctor came, but shook his head as he knelt beside the men. It was no use, for the cruel sea had drowned them.

The little boys turned and went out along the sands. Wilfred raised his head and took a deep breath of salt air, mixed with the scents of fish and tar, as he looked across the waters toward Wales, on the other side.

He loved the sea, and the sands, and he admired fishermen more than any other men in the world. Over there, in Wales, people were shopkeepers and miners, he thought scornfully. Here, where Wilfred Grenfell lived with his father, his mother, and his two brothers, people were adventurous. He decided now — at the age of five — in this year 1870, that he would be a fisherman. The sea took some — but he was sure that it would not take him!

The Grenfells lived near the town of Chester, not far from Liverpool. At first Wilfred went to the school run by his father, who was also a minister in the Church of England. Then his father decided that the two older boys, who were constantly wandering away along the sands, playing in fishing boats and getting into mischief, should go elsewhere. They were sent to different schools — Algernon to Repton and Wilfred to Marlborough.

At Marlborough Wilfred, a merry, active boy, had to fight for his rights, and he achieved the admiring title of "The Beast" because he usually won his battles. He enjoyed athletics, and made more of a name for himself in sports than in his studies. School was fun too, for he liked the boys and they liked him, and yet he missed the sea and the sands, and the slow talk of fishermen.

When Wilfred was ready to leave school, he had to make a decision. His father had moved to London and become the chaplain of a big hospital. Wilfred's thoughts about what he would become were quite naturally concerned with the ministry. But he was also interested in medicine. Should he go on to Oxford to study, or should he go into a London hospital and become a doctor? As he put away his school jackets, his collections of butterflies and stones, and his cricket bats, he thought it over. Then he went home to his father and mother in London and told them that he was going to live with them and study medicine in the hospital where his father was chaplain.

The city, the hospital, and the classes that he entered at

London University presented a new world to Wilfred Grenfell. The hospital was the largest in the British Isles, and in the year 1883, the study of medicine was mainly a matter of learning first-hand from the doctors. The part of the city in which the hospital was located was the East End, where the slums were the worst in London. It was here that Jane Addams had seen the terrible sight of starving hands reaching for rotten vegetables on a Saturday night.

Many of his fellow students came from quiet towns in other parts of England, and the brawling, evil influences of the slums had a bad effect on their characters. These things did not bother young Grenfell. He was the son of a minister, and he lived at home, although that home was in the slum district. He began to work harder at his studies than ever before. And, for fun, he helped organize football teams among students and joined the rowing crew of the University, on the Thames River.

When his father died and his mother went to live with relatives outside London, Wilfred moved into an apartment with two other students. In summer he went to the seashore, for the salt water was still home to him, and his happiest times were spent

73

in boats. He and his roommates began to get together groups of slum boys and to take them to the shore for camping trips on the sands. Boys who had never seen the fields and woods and salt water came back to London in the autumn healthier and happier.

In dark days of winter, when fog came down under chimney pots and swirled in brown clouds through the streets, Wilfred Grenfell learned the ways of the poor. In the hospital, day after day, he saw the terrible results of poverty. Men, women, and children were brought in suffering from illnesses and injuries caused by crime, starvation, and heavy drinking of gin and rum. Yet he learned that there was much good and friendliness in these people, no matter how low they had come to be.

Some of Grenfell's friends became fashionable doctors, but he was not interested in that kind of life. In 1886, he passed his examinations and became Dr. Grenfell. More than any others, he still liked seafaring men and enjoyed talking to every fisherman patient who came to the hospital. He heard of the months spent on the water by thousands of fishermen who went out for herring to the Dogger Bank in the far North Sea. These fishing boats sailed in great fleets and remained out for months, sending the fish back by fast cutters. Through long periods of dangerous weather the men stayed on the sea, their only entertainment a few hours on a grog, or saloon, ship. Here they lost their wages as fast as they received them. When they were sick, or injured, as often happened, they were sent to port on the cutters. Since there were no doctors with the fleet, many died on the way home.

Grenfell joined in plans for a floating hospital and mission for the fishing fleets. One cold and stormy January day he sailed

to the Dogger Bank. There were more than twenty thousand men and boys in the herring fleets, on ships that were often covered with ice or snow for the entire voyage. It took courage to go out to a vessel in a small boat in rough seas, to set a leg or doctor a wound. But the medical and mission ship was a great success. Gradually grog vessels began to lose more and more money, until finally they stopped going out altogether. Fishermen returned to port in better health, and with their wages.

From his fishermen friends young Dr. Grenfell heard talk of the fleets that went each year all the long way to the bleak coast of Labrador. Lying north and east of Canada, Labrador was a wild, cold land where only a few fisherfolk, Eskimos, and Indians lived. In all Labrador there was no doctor. Dr. Grenfell felt a deep urge to go there with the fishermen. He searched around until he found a little ship that he could buy, and a captain and mate to help him sail it. It was called the *Albert,* and was about the same size as the fifteenth-century vessel that the famous explorer, John Cabot, had sailed along the same sea route in 1497.

The *Albert* reached St. John's Harbour, Newfoundland, just

in time to see the town swept by the flames of a devastating fire, and just in time for the doctor to rush ashore to help the injured. Wilfred Grenfell never forgot the quiet courage of these people, who scarcely allowed the smoking ruins of their town to cool before they started rebuilding it. The *Albert* was soon off again, following the fishing fleet to the north along the rocky shores of Labrador. As the doctor's ship dropped anchor in Domino Run, flags were run up on the fleet's masts, and patients in need of help were already heading for the *Albert* in small boats.

When he stopped to realize that he was the only doctor, Dr. Grenfell felt a bit overwhelmed by his job. As the *Albert* bounced about on swells, rolling in from the ocean, Grenfell realized that here was his place. Here he could do a great deal of good for people who had simple courage, humor, and spirit. Everyone was poor —the Eskimos who came down for the summers from icy lands farther north, the Indians who appeared silently from inland forests to fish on the coast, and the English fishermen.

A Moravian mission had been established in Labrador, but it was small, and in spite of the unselfish work of Moravian ministers, not many people could be educated there. The need for medical care was great. Grenfell decided to return the following summer, and to bring another young doctor to help him.

There were many who needed that help. Labrador waters were fished in summer by fishermen from England, Canada, Newfoundland, and the United States. They came for herring, cod, halibut, and whales in the warm months, and for seal hunting on the ice floes in the bitter cold of winter. People always seemed to be moving about in Labrador. Although Labrador is no farther

north than England, it has a cold that is more severe than Lapland
and other arctic regions.

Nothing discouraged Dr. Grenfell. He liked Labrador, and
he returned each summer with other doctors and more help. After
a few years of summer voyages, he worked out a scheme to build
a hospital on the rocky shores of Labrador. He had not yet spent
a winter there. Instead of doing so, he had to leave for a speaking
tour to raise money for the hospital. His friend, Dr. Willway,
offered to stay in Labrador for a winter to find out what arctic
cold conditions were like.

In the spring, when Grenfell returned, he did not know
whether he would find his friend alive or frozen in his small house
at Battle Harbor. But Dr. Willway, healthy and cheerful, strode
out to greet him. The hospital was built, and from then on Dr.
Grenfell also spent his winters there whenever possible. From time
to time he went on other long speaking tours through the British
Isles, Europe, and the United States. Everywhere he told people
of the Eskimos, of the land of ice and snow, and of the fisherfolk.
More and more money came in. Dr. Grenfell was able to enlarge
his hospital at Battle Harbor, add a larger staff of doctors and

nurses, and then to build another hospital farther north.

Labrador was a cruel land where people were often killed or died of starvation. When children were left without help of any kind, somebody always brought them to the doctor. An orphanage was necessary, and when it was started, it grew and grew. Teachers offered to help, and nurses and doctors came during the summers without pay to assist the now famous doctor of Labrador.

Somehow salt water always seemed to be present in the important events of the life of Wilfred Grenfell. In 1909 he married Anne MacClanahan, an American, whom he had met on shipboard while returning from England. She was an adventurous girl, as much interested in the people of Labrador as her husband. She went to live with him near the hospital in St. Anthony. Their three children — Wilfred, Kinloch, and Rosamund — were born there. The Grenfells worked well together, and Anne soon proved that she could do many things that her doctor husband could not do. She could bring order to their work, and she could organize details and help with the important affairs of the International Grenfell Society, which had members all over the world. When Dr. Grenfell traveled about, speaking, Anne sometimes went along, but usually she stayed in Labrador to keep things going well.

The doctor had patients living long distances from St. Anthony, and he made his rounds in winter as well as in summer. Sometimes, in spring, he went with an expedition from St. John's to hunt seals. This was always an exciting voyage. He arrived at the port in time to see the sealers coming in by hundreds to sign up. The whole harbor was filled with sealing vessels, waiting to sail.

78

Sealing was subject to strict laws, and the fleet was not permitted to sail until two o'clock on March 10. Then, under the clear light skies of northern spring, the ships set sail. Whooping, shouting, and singing, sealers crowded the rails, and the fleet was off to the icy stretches where hunters risked their necks every hour on the treacherous "ice pans."

No other man was as popular as the doctor. He set broken legs, treated those who suffered the agonies of snow blindness, and cared for the victims of all sorts of accidents. One afternoon Dr. Grenfell, without asking permission of the captain, slipped over the side onto the ice and joined a group of seal hunters. He caught up with them just as a brisk wind, which had kept the chunks of ice together, died down. The ice drifted apart, leaving the little knot of men floating dangerously on an ice pan. To keep warm, they made a fire of the fat of seals that they had killed and moved about it, playing leapfrog, jumping, and running. They had to move fast and keep moving to prevent the deadly cold from killing them. When Dr. Grenfell and his companions were almost exhausted from fatigue and their little blaze was growing smaller, a watcher set up a whoop of joy. A dim bulk had loomed up on the

79

horizon. The ship was coming toward them!

The Labrador doctor was known from one end of this desolate land to the other. He had mastered the ways of the north and was respected for it. He had his own team of sled dogs — big, strong, tough animals. For many miles, as he went his rounds from town to lonely hut, the dogs were his only companions. He liked to tell people of the intelligence of his dogs. When the doctor unhitched his team, each dog curled up in deep snow to sleep, with nothing out of the cold white cover but a black nose and two ears. In the morning the dogs jumped up, shook the snow out of their thick fur, and frisked about like house dogs. The doctor drove his sled, called a *komatik*, along trails where he kept food hidden for his dogs, so that he would not have to carry it. Yet he knew that any man or woman in all of that country would starve, if necessary, to feed the "doctor's team."

The doctor's team, like other Eskimo dogs, never barked. They howled like their relatives, the wolves, and were even fiercer than wolves. His sled dogs were absolutely fearless and would attack a polar bear, the most ferocious animal of the north, when wolves would not.

As the years passed, the doctor seemed to grow more active, instead of less. Eskimos, known as the "little people," were his friends. He welcomed them in the early summer as they came to the hospital to have their teeth pulled or diseases treated. Dr. Grenfell saw, with sadness, that they frequently died of illnesses from which white men usually recovered without much trouble. Eskimos had always lived on raw seal meat and fish. He knew that the starchy diet of the settlements was not good for them.

Why did the people of Labrador have such a hard time to keep from starving? In this cold land the season was very short for growing things, and most food had to be brought in by traders. Skins and fish should pay enough to keep trappers and fishermen fed and clothed with a roof over them. Yet the people starved. Dr. Grenfell discovered that the reason was the "trucking" system. Traders who owned stores would not use money but, in return for skins or fish, would issue food. After a time the fisherman was always in debt to the storekeeper, and he had to take less for his fish than the catch was worth. What could be done?

Dr. Grenfell started a group of cooperative stores. This gave him some pretty bad headaches, for he was fought by the traders. But the doctor who had helped get rid of grog ships on the Dogger Bank was not going to be beaten. After a time the old system changed. Trappers and fishermen were able to get fair prices for their fish and skins, and were better able to stay out of debt.

The years brought honors to Dr. Grenfell. He was knighted by the king of England, and he and his wife became lord and lady. Yet none of the honors meant as much to him as the knowledge that the people of Newfoundland and Labrador had hospitals and schools and the chance for a good life. As long as he lived, he took an active part in the work of the hospital, and a great pride in the friendship of the doctors and nurses who came to help him.

Until Dr. Grenfell died in 1940, his home was on the bare, chilly shores of a northern land far from the Sands of Dee. But here, too, the salt wind swept inland, bringing a scent of ropes, tar, and fish, and overhead gray gulls circled, screaming and crying their sea-bird songs.

# Great Soul

MAHATMA GANDHI

India is a land of hot sunlight, of gleaming temples, of water buffalo slowly pulling plows, and of brown people in white cotton garments crowding the noisy, odorous streets of cities. India is a place where enormous crowds gather to bathe in the sacred Ganges River, or to gain religious strength by seeing a holy man, or hearing him speak. India is a country where everything is decided by parents, religion, or custom for any small girl or boy.

From his birth in 1869, Mohandas Gandhi had his life laid out neatly for him. He was the youngest member of a family of father, mother, three boys, and two girls. They lived by religious rule, for the Hindu religion was very strict. They also lived by caste rule. A boy born into one caste could not change into another, and the Gandhi family was in the middle caste. They had to follow only certain trades or professions. A Hindu child was betrothed in babyhood, and was married when the father arranged the wedding.

At thirteen, Mohandas felt very old, for this was 1882, and it was to be the year of his marriage. His oldest brother was already married, and now Mohandas and his other brother and a cousin were to have a triple wedding before many months had passed. But, as he stood in the doorway of his home with his brother and sisters, he looked very young. They all stared anxiously up at the sky. Would Mother have dinner today, or not?

Their mother was even more religious than most Hindus. She was undergoing a fast now, one in which she had vowed not to eat unless she saw the sun just before mealtime. Although nearly every day was sunny, somehow each time as she sat down at the table the sun disappeared behind a cloud.

Suddenly Mohandas cried, "Mother, come quickly. The sun!" His mother walked slowly to the doorway, as the maid placed food upon the table. Just as she reached the door, the sun was swept out of sight behind a cloud. Mohandas could have wept in disappointment, for he could see that his mother had grown thin during the fast. But she only smiled, and said calmly, "It does not matter. God did not want me to eat today."

Her children always remembered that day, for it impressed upon them that their mother was a saintly woman. Father was honest and truthful, and his opinion was held in high regard at court as well as in the town. He was, however, rather short-tempered.

In spite of their respect for their mother's religion, the boys grew up resentful of the strict religious rules of their household. Other boys who lived in Hindu homes could smoke and did not have to go without meat or to fast on special days. Once Mohandas had eaten meat secretly with a school friend, but his conscience hurt him so badly that he did not try it again.

Mohandas felt a great respect for his father, even when he

disobeyed him, and he had a firm loyalty to the brother who was just a little older than he. They were companions, and when his brother began to gamble, Mohandas felt that, somehow, he must help keep this from their father. His brother had been given an arm band of pure gold by their father. He persuaded Mohandas to cut a strip off and sell it. This Mohandas did, but afterwards his nights were horrible with guilty dreams, and he was sick with remorse. Pale with worry, he wrote out a confession and gave it to his father. When his father read it, he cried and tears came to Mohandas' eyes. He made up his mind that truth was the most important principle in life, and that he would never again take part in deceit.

The marriage of three young boys to three little girls meant a great deal of expense for their families, for this day must be one of gay festivity. Together the three boys and their child brides took the seven steps in the Hindu ceremony, and ate of the sacred sweetmeats. Then, after days of feasting, the boys brought their brides to live in their fathers' houses, and went back to the routine of day school and work.

When Mohandas was sixteen his father died. Mohandas was a devoted son, who cared for his father in his last illness, and who grieved for a long time after his death. The Hindu religion, always so important in the Gandhi family, came to mean even more to Mohandas. He believed in its emphasis on complete truth, on simple kindness to others, and on respect for all living things. He believed that nonviolence was the right way of life for all men.

His mother and brothers had respect for Mohandas' brilliant young mind, and they wished him to go to college to study law. Since such studies required a longer time to complete in India than in England, they advised him to take the long journey. So one day, years later, Mohandas said good-by to his mother and family and to his wife and son, and went aboard a ship at Bombay. This was a big step for a young Indian to take, for England was a strange and a faraway place.

For hundreds of years India had been an English colony and many Indians wanted independence for their country. Mohandas had this feeling too, but he was only nineteen years old, and knew nothing as yet of the world outside his own part of vast India.

In England, although he was lonely and poor, Mohandas managed to live and learn. When he left there three years later he could speak English well and he had been admitted to the bar

88

as a lawyer. He had also made a few friends. And he had gained
a new sympathy for Christianity, impossible to him in India,
where he had resented foreign missionaries. Gandhi had read
the New Testament and had come to admire the teachings of
Jesus.

Mohandas Gandhi returned to India expecting to practice
law there. When, however, after several years' experience at home,
he was offered a good place in an Indian law firm in South Africa,
he decided to take it. Leaving his wife and son once more, Gandhi
sailed for Africa. His arrival on the coast of that continent and
his journey inland by train were experiences he never forgot.
Both the English and the Dutch who ran different South African
states disliked people of a darker skin. Gandhi was treated rudely,
and although he had a first-class ticket, he was forced to travel
third class in the train. All of the Indians there told him of their
troubles. Although Gandhi had an important position in the
law firm, he made up his mind to help his fellow Indians.

After a while Mrs. Gandhi and their son came to Africa.
They went to Johannesburg to live, and their second son was born
there. During the Boer War, when the English were fighting the

Dutch, Gandhi organized a Red Cross unit, enlisted his Indian friends, and did valuable work saving lives under fire.

During these years Gandhi read the books of Leo Tolstoy, a Russian count who had given up court life under the czar to live as a peasant on one of his estates. Tolstoy believed that a farm colony in which everyone worked with his hands for the good of all was the right way to live. Gandhi decided to start such a colony. He bought a farm, placed on it a number of people who wished to live and work on the land, and called it the Phoenix Settlement. Later Gandhi, with his wife and two sons, went there to live also. He brought with him very strict ideas about food. His religious belief did not permit the eating of meat, and in addition to that he began to think that simple food was important to clear thinking and clean living.

Gandhi also became editor of an Indian newspaper, published at first in Johannesburg, and then later at the settlement. Indians in the Phoenix colony were more fortunate than those in Johannesburg, where they had to stay in a part of the city without sanitation and live in huts. Gandhi's newspaper constantly carried on a campaign to try to improve conditions for Indians.

When the terrible black plague broke out in a gold mine where some Indians worked, it spread to their slum in the city. Gandhi went at once to organize efforts to take care of the stricken, and to prevent the further spread of the disease. All of the people in his law office went with him. They got a doctor, put the patients in one house, and nursed them. Although twenty Indians died, others did not catch the disease, and it did not affect the rest of the city.

In 1908, fighting broke out in a part of Africa called Natal. Gandhi and his followers once again took charge of a hospital unit and gave valuable service to the British army. Although he did not believe in violence, he did believe in helping those in need. During these years Gandhi developed his own unique method of working for better conditions and more freedom for his own people. From childhood his religion had taught him to believe in nonviolence. What Gandhi now did was to apply this principle to political problems. He advanced the doctrine of non-violent resistance to laws that he thought unjust. This he taught his friends, and the number of his followers grew during the years in South Africa.

The Indians, under Gandhi, refused to obey unfair laws that denied them their basic liberties. Gandhi said that it was noble to go to prison for liberty, and not to resist, no matter what happened. This he did himself, and when arrested went to jail quietly, without anger. His wife went to prison also, along with some other women, and Indian women began to believe that they should struggle for justice and freedom side by side with the men.

This policy of resistance finally accomplished most of the

91

things that Gandhi had wanted it to do, and the worst laws were changed. Gandhi had become a man known to the world for his principles and his courage. He decided to take his family home to India, where he thought that he could be of more use to his countrymen than was possible in Africa.

In December, 1914, when war was raging in Europe, the Gandhis returned to their country. The people of the Phoenix Settlement went to India also. While they were building up the colony there, Gandhi set himself to study the problems of India. He spent a year of travel, learning the conditions under which people lived. He became convinced that India must become an independent nation. Yet his belief in nonviolent resistance was stronger than ever. To him, and to his followers, this was the answer to the question of how to win freedom for India. Gandhi now became the leader in a campaign that was to last throughout most of his life, and was to end in an independent Indian government.

Gandhi counseled the people to oppose British rule and to resist without violence. They were to go to jail if necessary, but were not to obey unjust laws. He asked his people, who looked on him now as a holy man, to refuse to use English goods. From one end of India to the other, people responded. Wherever Gandhi went, he was called the Mahatma, for mahatma means Great Soul. Thousands came for many miles just to look at him. All over the country Indians were beginning to believe that they would add to their own spiritual worth by hearing him speak.

Yet, when time came for quiet, calm disobedience, without violence, some behaved differently. Hatred of the English was

intense, and crowds rioted in several districts, causing injury and death to many. Mahatma Gandhi, who had never intended to start a violent struggle, and who did not believe in forceful resistance, was held responsible by the English authorities. He felt that he really was to blame, for he had taught disobedience without being able to teach self-control. He took to fasting, going without food for weeks, until many feared for his life. And then he was arrested by the authorities. Quietly he went to prison, where he was always treated kindly and with respect, and where he spent his time studying and writing.

Gandhi believed in the ways of age-old Indian life. He did not think that modern machinery and Western power and enterprise would help India. So he asked his followers to wear the simple white cotton garments of ancient India, not machine-made Western clothing. He himself learned to spin cotton cloth, and he taught others to do so, rather than to buy English goods. Gandhi lived a very simple personal life. He never ate meat but existed chiefly on goat's milk, fruits, and nuts.

Yet the Mahatma believed that some of the traditional Indian ways should be changed. Below the lowest caste there is a large group of people without caste. They are called "untouchables" and they cannot mix with others. All over India Gandhi saw thousands of these very poor people, who had to live almost like stray animals because they were "untouchables." This seemed wrong to him, and so he began a campaign to break down the barrier in India. Into his home he took several "untouchable" orphan children, and he asked some other outcasts to live in the farm colony. This brought violent criticism of the Mahatma

94

from high-caste people, while the majority of the Indians loved him and followed his leadership. Now the government of India has outlawed "untouchability," although high-caste Indians still call the no-caste Indians "unclean."

In the struggle for independence Gandhi was the principal leader for a long time. Then the country turned to others, who believed in bringing India up to date by starting factories and working for modern improvements. Yet Gandhi, sitting beside his spinning wheel, was still a spiritual leader and, to many, a saintly man.

The problems of India were many. The country is made up of different groups of races, of different states, and of different religions. Hindus live in India, and so do Buddhists and Mohammedans. Often the Mohammedans, or Moslems, and the Hindus fought each other in riots that broke out in the streets from time to time. The Mahatma continued, in spite of all these events, to teach nonviolence, along with stubborn resistance to the English. Because of this opposition Gandhi went to prison several times. His longest sentence was ended when he became very ill with appendicitis.

Two years after the end of World War II Gandhi was living quietly in the "untouchable" quarter in Delhi, the capital of India. The long struggle for independence had been won and England had just turned over the government to the Indians. At the same time Pakistan, formerly a part of India, was established as an independent Moslem state. Gandhi had helped in the negotiations for independence from England, and was blamed by some people for allowing Pakistan to go.

While Indians celebrated, the Mahatma spent his time praying, fasting, and spinning. Then riots broke out between the Hindus and the Moslems. Homes were destroyed and men murdered. Gandhi moved into the ruined Moslem section of Calcutta. He said that he would not leave until his people made peace. Many angry Hindus and Moslems protested violently against him. His own followers could do nothing.

One day as the Mahatma sat spinning, his head bowed as his fingers moved, several wild young men burst into the room. They shouted, "Get out of the Moslem quarter! Get out!"

The Mahatma raised his head and, in the serene voice that he always used, said, "If you want to take me out of here, you must take me as a corpse."

The young men looked at each other, and a silence fell on the bare room. Without another word they turned and went out,

96

their heads down, as if ashamed. After that, the riots stopped, and groups of Hindus and groups of Moslems paraded up and down the streets of Calcutta with banners calling for peace. The spirit of the Great Soul had prevailed again, through calm courage and the quiet strength of conviction.

Disorders sprang up in other parts of India. As fast as peace came to one place, violence seemed to appear in another. Gandhi went from place to place. Then he returned to Delhi to conduct a protest campaign of prayer meetings. He began a fast, going without food day after day as he prayed for peace. He was seventy-eight years old, and many believed that he would die from this starvation. Newspapers all over the world were writing of it, and throughout India people talked of little else. They paraded the streets with banners promising peace if the Mahatma would end his fast. Talk of war between India and Pakistan stopped. Pledges of peace were made by the heads of both the Hindu and the Moslem organizations, and the great Mahatma broke his fast.

Gandhi was so weak that he could not walk when he began a prolonged prayer meeting in the garden of the home where he was staying. He was carried to it each evening in a chair. But he gradually gained strength until, on January 30, he was able to walk to his chair in the garden, for a meeting to which the public was invited, as always.

As he walked across the grass to his seat, a number of people closed in about him. Abruptly the peaceful silence was shattered by a shot. Those around the Mahatma were frozen with surprise, and then they pushed forward in confusion, crying out. On the grass Gandhi lay dead, assassinated by a fellow Indian. A vast crowd assembled before the house, and Mr. Nehru, the Prime Minister of India, came to speak to the weeping people.

Next day the body of Mahatma Gandhi was cremated, according to Indian religious custom, on the wide plain beside the river near Delhi, and his ashes were distributed, on the thirteenth day, to the seven sacred rivers of India.

The place of Mahatma Gandhi in history is twofold. He is honored as a man who helped more than any other to achieve freedom for the Indian nation. And he is not only regarded as a holy man in India, but is respected everywhere as a religious scholar and spiritual leader.

# Jungle Doctor

## ALBERT SCHWEITZER

The old Lutheran church looked very high to a small boy sitting quietly in a dim pew, waiting for his father, Pastor Schweitzer, to come to the pulpit to preach. All around him Sunday garments rustled, yet if he moved so much as a finger his mother put a firm hand on his arm. Albert fixed his eyes intently on the organ. Would the Devil appear today? Now his father had finished his sermon, and his prayer. Suddenly there it was — a bearded face above the organ. Albert stiffened with fright, for who could it be but the Devil himself? The wonderful organ music swelled and grew until it filled the church with heavenly sounds. Albert forgot the Devil face. He felt almost faint with the music.

As he grew older, Albert came to know that the strange bearded face was not the Devil, but was a mirrored reflection of the organist, kindly Father Iltis. But his feeling about organ music never changed.

Albert Schweitzer felt that he was born to like music. His mother's family was talented and was also skilled at building church organs. Most of the men were pastors like his father. Albert, who was one of five children, was born in 1875 in Alsace-

101

Lorraine, that fought-over land that was both German and French in language and population. His home was the pleasant parsonage in the village of Günsbach, in a lovely rolling farm country. His was a happy childhood in a family that shared the same interests, and loved music and the church.

He had friends in the village, too, and because he did not like to seem different, he insisted on wearing the clothing of the peasant lads instead of the more dignified clothes of the parson's son. Yet, although he liked his friends and wanted to be with them, he found it difficult sometimes to enter into their sports. One day in early spring he went out into the fields with a friend to hunt birds with a slingshot. As they walked along, Albert was hoping that they would not find any birds. Suddenly his companion whispered, "Look, a whole flock!" Albert, quivering all over at the thought of killing any creature, held his sling off balance so that he would miss.

As he stood there, watching his friend aim his stone carefully at the little birds picking at the grain, Albert heard church bells ringing sweetly over the fields. To him they seemed to say, "Thou shalt not kill!" Albert threw down his slingshot and shouted loudly to frighten the birds away. As they whirred up into the safety of the blue sky and disappeared, he knew that he no longer cared if his friends made fun of him. He knew that he could not kill any living thing as a sport; that he would never kill except as a matter of absolute necessity.

Albert's interest in music grew rapidly. He tried to play the piano at home, and he listened happily to the singing of groups who enjoyed the folk songs of the region. When he was old

102

enough, he entered the Lycee school in Mulhouse and went to live with his Uncle Louis and Aunt Sophie, who had no children. Uncle Louis was director of the school. Albert lived in Mulhouse eight years, and there progressed from a country boy who had at first had trouble learning to a good student. He also made such rapid growth in musical skill that his teacher was astonished.

At fifteen Albert was permitted to play the church organ, and his teacher, the organist, soon began giving him regular times to play during the services. When he was eighteen, he entered the University of Strasbourg to take up religious studies, for he had decided to become a pastor. Music was still intensely important to him. It was about this time that on a trip to Paris he met Charles Marie Widor, the organist of the cathedral of St. Sulpice. They became lifetime friends at once, even though Albert returned later to Strasbourg. He remained there for many years, first as a student and then as a teacher.

The greatest decision of his life was made when Albert Schweitzer was twenty-one years old. He was very happy in his studies and his music, with his friends and his family. Yet the miserable lot of so many other less fortunate people was continually in his thoughts. He began to believe that he must pay for his good fortune by devoting himself to others. Albert Schweitzer deliberately decided to devote the next ten years to religious studies and to music and, after that, to work for the rest of his life to relieve the suffering of others.

Like Benjamin Franklin, and like John Wesley, he organized his time. Schweitzer was a large man, of great energy, both mentally and physically. He began to plan his hours of work, his studies, writing, teaching, and music. He made a special study of Johann Sebastian Bach's music, and it was not long before he was recognized as a distinguished Bach authority, as well as a talented performer of Bach's music. Then he became widely known as a religious scholar. He lived in Paris for a time and studied music there with his friend Widor and others. He published religious treatises that attracted even wider scholarly attention.

When Schweitzer was thirty-one, and was already distinguished in the fields of theology and music, he quietly entered a medical school to prepare himself to be a doctor. His relatives and friends argued with him, for they were aghast at this decision. How could such a brilliant man as Schweitzer throw away his opportunities? It was hard to believe that he would really do so. But now the scholar and musician became a medical student having some trouble learning these new and difficult subjects. One day Schweitzer had seen a statue of an African Negro, and he had stood before it a long time. The stories that he heard from missionaries and doctors were tales of the horrors of disease in

Africa, where many native tribesmen had no medical help whatever.

Albert Schweitzer decided to devote his life to the people in the jungles of Africa. In 1912, he resigned his position as teacher of religion and as pastor, which he had kept up while studying medicine. That summer he married Helene Bresslau, daughter of a professor, a girl who understood his talents and his need for service to humanity. They planned to go to Africa together, and Helene undertook training as a nurse. Dr. Schweitzer went out to build a hospital at Lambaréné, on the River Ogowe, in a hot tropical forest. He was sent the first time by a French missionary society, but only after he had promised to work as a doctor and not as a pastor. The society disagreed sharply with his religious views, and he promised to be "silent as a carp" on religion.

In 1913, the doctor and his wife sailed for Africa, along with baggage that was mostly made up of medical supplies. Albert Schweitzer and his wife traveled from the coast up a strange river, winding through mysterious forests. In the water herds of rhinoceroses wallowed, and crocodiles, thrusting their snouts out of the mud, looked like knotty floating logs. On shore, there were wild elephants that sometimes trampled native villages to ruins, and at night the darkness was pierced with the cry of lion or jackal. Here, a mile from the mission church by river canoe, the Schweitzers built their rough hospital. At first it was one shack, and then it grew as the doctor labored day after day with his hands. He gradually gathered natives to help, and after a while he became a man who could lead and direct others, as well as a scholar and musician.

In the next few years the hospital became a small village. Natives heard of it and traveled great distances to be treated. With each new patient there came a whole family to camp in the clearing. The doctor had to give food to them all, and so he had the women cook for their sick relatives and bring food to their beds. This was not the white, starched hospital of a city in America or Europe. Dr. Schweitzer fought his way patiently through many difficult and strange problems. Then, just as he was beginning to believe that his work was going to be permanent, fighting broke out in Europe.

In 1914, France and Germany were at war. Lambaréné was in part of the French African territory. The Schweitzers were of German extraction, and came from the German part of Alsace. At first they were kept under watch at Lambaréné by the French government and continued their work as before. Then, with only a couple of hours' notice, the French government ordered the Schweitzers to be sent to an internment camp in France. They hurriedly packed instruments and other valuables and locked them up, and went down the river to go aboard ship for Bordeaux. On shipboard Dr. Schweitzer was not allowed to speak to anyone except his wife, and so he occupied his time by working on a manuscript and by learning some Bach music by heart.

In the prison in Bordeaux the Schweitzers made friends with

many unfortunate people who were in desperate need of help such as could be offered by a minister and a doctor. For Albert Schweitzer the most difficult thing about the prison was lack of work. So, in addition to giving all of the medical aid that he was allowed to give to the other inmates, he began to practice music every day on an old wooden table. Here he would sit for hours, as if at the piano or the organ. He practiced from memory with his fingers, at the same time going over the music in his mind. Thus Schweitzer, the lover of music, did not allow himself to forget, and as for Schweitzer the scholar—he was lucky enough to have the manuscript of a book that he had begun, and he worked on this, too.

After a while the doctor and his wife were sent to another prison, in southern France. It was located in a building that had been an insane asylum. Here they discovered that this was where, thirty years before, the famous Vincent van Gogh had done some of his best paintings while he was a patient. In 1918, not long before the end of the war, friends in Paris arranged to have Dr. and Mrs. Schweitzer sent to Switzerland. Then, after the Armistice had silenced the guns, they went home to Günsbach and to Strasbourg. In the autumn of 1919, their daughter, Rhena, was born. During the following years Dr. Schweitzer wrote on religious subjects, traveled about giving concerts and lectures, and received a number of honorary degrees.

Yet he was always sure that he would return to his work in Africa. Mrs. Schweitzer was not well, for her health had suffered in prison. So in 1924, when he sailed again, he went without her. A young doctor accompanied him, and a nurse soon followed.

108

When he arrived at Lambaréné, Dr. Schweitzer saw that the clearing was overgrown and that the jungle had claimed his hospital buildings. He decided to build a new hospital village on an island in the river. This time the huts were larger, better made, and stronger. Money was a real problem, for such a project had to have many supplies.

Other doctors and nurses came to help. Dr. Schweitzer seemed to be everywhere at once, directing, healing, and working with his hands. He imported a herd of goats to supply milk. The goats climbed up on the roofs of the hospital huts and scrambled about as if they were on their native mountain peaks. There were other strange problems. A goat on the roof was not as bad as an elephant in a banana grove, breaking down delicate trees. There were mosquitoes to be fought, and the disease malaria, carried by mosquitoes, was always with them. Almost every native suffered from it.

The Negroes of this region had little food and, until the hospital came, no medical treatment. They spoke many different tribal languages and believed in strange superstitions. The doctor took care of them all, with the help of medical men and nurses

109

who came out to give their time and energy to the work. Sleeping sickness was a problem, and other diseases, strange to people in America and Europe, killed and maimed the natives. Two of these were elephantiasis and leprosy. Unlike Father Damien, Dr. Schweitzer was a doctor, and he lived in an age when new drugs and more knowledge of leprosy could cure or help the patient.

In 1927, Dr. Schweitzer left Africa again for a visit with his wife and daughter, who were living in the Black Forest in Germany. Old Pastor Schweitzer and his wife had died, and Dr. Schweitzer now had no family home in Günsbach. He began to travel again, giving concerts and lectures. The money that he made went to the hospital work in Lambaréné. Everywhere people were talking of this extraordinary man and of his hospital in the jungles. Money began to come in for the work, and an organization was formed, with headquarters in Günsbach. The doctor built a home in his own Alsatian village. His wife, daughter, and Madame Martin, who handled the work of the hospital organization, were established there. This home the doctor paid for with money that he received from the Goethe Prize, given in honor of the famous German writer. Dr. Schweitzer received it for his scholarship and for "his general services to humanity."

On his return to Lambaréné, Dr. Schweitzer began to write his autobiography, which was published in 1931. Then he spent two years at his jungle hospital before returning to Europe again. Now Dr. Schweitzer was independent of the French missionary society. The missionaries had not been able to return after the war, so Dr. Schweitzer began to preach to the natives every Sun-

day morning. He was writing also, and he never failed to play his piano each day. The piano had been given to him by friends in the Bach Society in Paris. This piano had been especially made of metal to prevent the termites from ruining it. And every evening at sunset patients, nurses, and relatives of the sick paused in their work, to sit in silence, listening to the music made by their doctor.

One of the books written by Dr. Schweitzer was on Indian religions. He had met Mahatma Gandhi and was greatly interested in his beliefs. Dr. Schweitzer had his own basic principle, and this he called "a reverence for life." He could recall his feeling as he heard the church bells chime out in Günsbach, when he had scared the birds away from danger. His belief in preserving, protecting, and healing all living things was evident in all that he did and said.

In 1939, when he was once again in Strasbourg and Günsbach, the doctor realized that again war was threatening. This time he did not want to see his hospital deserted and ruined. Suddenly Dr. Schweitzer left for Africa, even though he had to break engagements to do so. This time he remained at Lambaréné for seven years, and this time the war and the fighting reached his jungle wilderness. Although French Africa was involved, both sides spared the hospital, and Madame Schweitzer,

111

who had left her married daughter in Switzerland, was able to join her husband.

At the end of the war a great interest in Dr. Schweitzer's work began to spread throughout the world. Money came in from America to make it possible to extend the hospital work. The doctor built a separate village for patients who had leprosy, away from the other hospital. Young doctors and nurses came to help, and the hospital received new equipment. In 1948, Dr. Schweitzer went back once more to Europe for a visit, for concerts, and to lecture. He had the joy of seeing his grandchildren in Switzerland and of getting to know his daughter's husband, who was an organ builder in Zurich.

Every time that he returned to Europe, Dr. Schweitzer made it a point to find an old church organ, sometimes more than one, that was in need of cleaning and repairs. These things he did himself, from love of the work. One of his friends said that the doctor "saved old Negroes in Africa and old organs in Europe." Honors were pouring in on him as he grew older. He was given the Nobel Peace Prize, and his music was put on records. His books were well known to scholars in colleges all over the world.

The jungle doctor, in 1957, eighty-two years old, remains a kindly man who can enforce his hospital rules sternly for the good of all. Like many others who have given a lifetime of service without a thought of reward, he has received the only reward that means anything to him. To Dr. Schweitzer this reward is the knowledge that he has been of service to those who need him. He has truly dedicated his talents and his labors to "reverence for life."